Published and Created by Making Memories®
Executive Director: Paula Chen Su
Creative Director of Publications: Gail Pierce-Watne
Associate Editor: Jayme Shepherd
Art Directors: Anthony Hadden and Kevin Thompson
Designer: Doug Seely
Writer: Jennifer Kofford
Photographer: Skylar Nielsen
Photographer's Assistant: Angie Hancock

For information about bulk sales or promotional pricing, please contact Customer Service at 1.800.286.5263 or customerservice@makingmemories.com.

Printed in the USA.

ISBN 1-893352-15-3

PaperCachet

PAPERCRAFTING | CARDMAKING | SCRAPBOOKING

You know when you've got it. And if you don't have it, you want it. That little something that makes your layouts, cards and papercrafts meaningful, memorable and simply amazing. It's called cachet. And it's what you'll give any and all kinds of paper when you use the dozens of innovative and inspiring techniques you'll find throughout the pages of this book. It's a little elusive but definitely essential—and it's all right here. Enjoy!

Contents

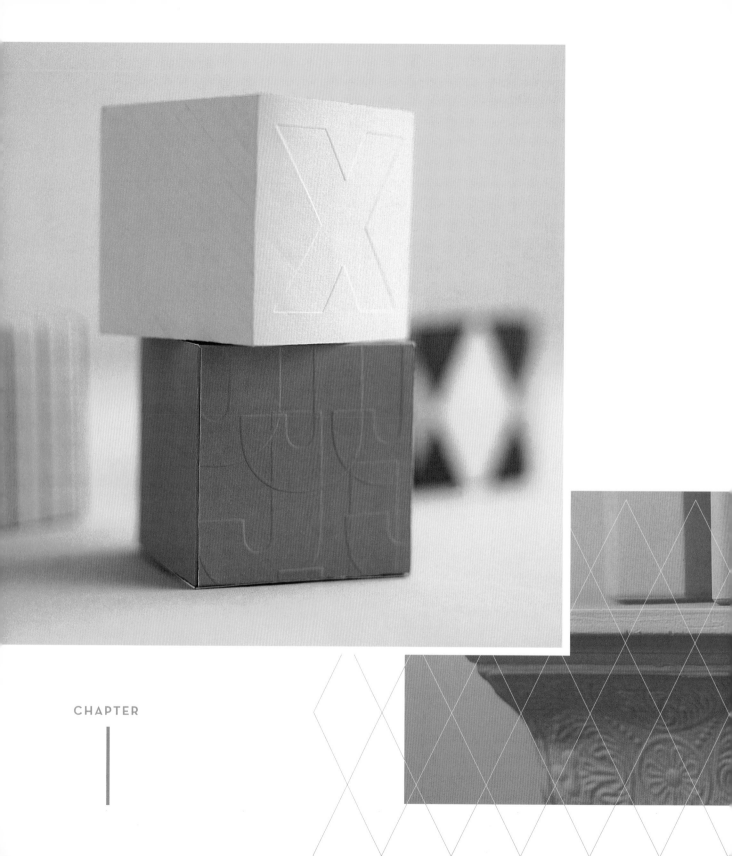

CHAPTER

You've only got one chance to make a stellar first impression. Naturally, one way your pages can do it is with embossing. Use a variety of store-bought templates, experiment with your stash of metal embellishments or make custom templates to fit your individual projects. And when you really want to heat things up, get out the powder and heat gun. No matter what technique you try, you'll definitely make your mark.

KISS ME, YOU FOOL
by Erin Terrell

Blossoms, cosmopolitan
embellishment paper,
gameboard alphabet,
like it is, mini brads and ribbon:
Making Memories
Computer font: Incognitype

how to: Trim harlequin or other patterned paper to size and emboss lines along the pattern. For an easy straight-line embossing template, line paper up with the grooves in a paper trimmer and run stylus along grooves. Emboss three straight lines along edge of bottom border and a single line around all edges of accent blocks.

THANKS
by Wendy Anderson

Classic small card base, cosmo ribbon,
cosmopolitan embellishment paper,
decorative brad, distressing kit,
eyelet charms, metal word and mini
brads: Making Memories

how to: Secure metal word and eyelet charm flower shapes to light table and use as embossing
templates on patterned and solid sides of Cosmopolitan paper. Lightly sand raised edges to
expose paper fibers. Lightly ink or chalk over surfaces to age. Use a variety of Decorative Brads
and mini brads to create flower centers.

ALL YOURS
By Loni Stevens

Computer fonts:
AL Uncle Charles downloaded from
www.twopeasinabucket.com and
Hootie downloaded from the Internet

Embossing templates: Lasting
Impressions and Staples

Jump rings, metal frame, mini brads,
patterned cardstock, ribbon, staples
and woven label:
Making Memories

Keyhole brad: 7Gypsies

Paper: Bazzill Basics

Punch: Marvy Uchida

Stencil: Duro Decal Co.

Tab: KI Memories

Texture templates: Fiskars

Other: Flowers and ribbon

how to: With double-lined template, emboss around edges of background. Create three monochromatic blocks using a variety of embossing techniques. Use Punched and Embossed Backgrounds technique (see page 21) for the first block. On the second block, emboss letter on bottom left corner and small circles over remainder of surface. Create third block by embossing entire area with the same template. Attach journaling and embellishments to each square.

1. background

2. border

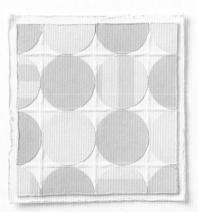

3. pattern

4. focal point

by Loni Stevens

1. Emboss the entire surface of a background and add stitching, ribbon and trim on top.

2. Emboss graduated circles down a strip of paper for a graphic border.

3. Punch shapes from cardstock, adhere to background and emboss horizontal and
vertical rows of straight lines to create a series of boxes.

4. Emboss pattern in patterned sticker and rub white glimmer chalk over surface to create a soft, shimmery look.

GIFT TAG
by Robyn Werlich

Bead chain, cosmopolitan embellishment paper, eyelet tag alphabet,
ribbon, staples, stitches and word
fetti: Making Memories
Embossing powder, pigment ink pad
and stamp: Stampin' Up!
Other: Ribbon

how to: Stamp flower with white pigment ink onto cardstock. Quickly sprinkle with
white embossing powder and heat emboss. Cut out flower shape, punch six holes in
the middle and thread ribbon through to create center. Place in the bottom right
corner of gift tag to embellish.

BIRTHDAY
by Charla Campbell

Acrylic paint: Folk Art

Defined, eyelet letter, jump rings, magnetic date stamp, ribbon, snap, stamping ink and upright slot card base: Making Memories

Embossing powder: JudiKins

Other: Embossing template and tag

how to: Cut cardstock to create insert, dry emboss dots over surface and dab raised areas with paint. Place Defined sticker along top edge and edge insert with paint. Sprinkle painted areas with embossing powder and heat emboss. Paint heart snap and a number from Eyelet Letter alphabet, sprinkle with embossing powder and heat emboss. Add a second coat of powder and heat again, if desired.

TREASURE JOURNAL
by Maggie Holmes

Charmed photo corner, cosmo ribbon,
cosmopolitan embellishment paper, decorative brad,
defined, fabric tape, foam stamps, ledger paper
and scrapbook colors acrylic paint: Making Memories
Embossing powder and stamping ink: Ranger Industries
Ribbon: Li'l Davis Designs
Watermark ink: VersaMark by Tsukineko
Other: Composition book, tulle and silk ribbon

how to: Cover front and back covers of composition
book with various papers, stickers, ribbon and
stamps and trim to fit. Place Fabric Tape along
binding to hide seams. Cut several flowers in
graduating sizes from Cosmopolitan paper, dab
with watermark ink, sprinkle with embossing
powder and heat. Layer together, adding tulle,
ribbon and Decorative Brad to secure and attach
to front cover.

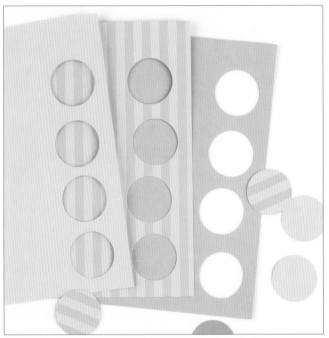

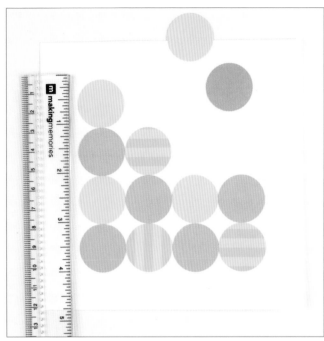

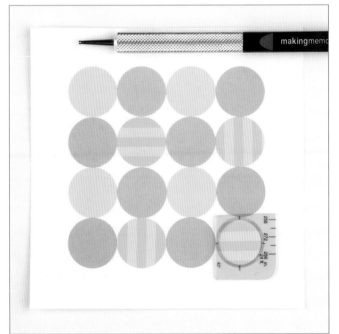

PUNCHED AND EMBOSSED BACKGROUNDS

1. With a circle punch, punch 16 circles from three coordinating sheets of cardstock.

2. Arrange circles on background, mixing patterns and shades and attach. Use a ruler as a guide, if necessary.

3. Flip piece over and, using a light box and a circle template that measures slightly smaller than the punched circles, rub through template with stylus to emboss. Circles will be raised with a border around the edges. Repeat embossing on all circles.

ABCD

You spent all those hours in grade school mastering your ABCs and 123s. Now make them fabulous. It's simple—just try an unique printing technique, cut out custom letters and coat them with lacquer or alter store-bought alphabets. Perfect for creating titles, journaling, monograms and accents, your projects will be full of letters and numbers that will make the grade.

LETTERS

LOVE YOU
by Janet Hopkins

Computer font: Elephant downloaded from the Internet

Patterned cardstock, rub-ons mini, scrapbook colors acrylic paint
and upright window card base: Making Memories

Toggle clasp: Westrim Crafts

Other: Jewelry tag and ribbon

how to: Layer strips of patterned cardstock in various widths
together and trim to fit front of card. Cut out window opening
with craft knife and stitch around edges to secure strips. Print
letter to fit opening, cut out and paint. When dry, apply rub-on.
Adhere to square of patterned cardstock and attach inside card
so that letter is visible through opening when card is closed.
Complete greeting by printing onto jewelry tag and tying to
ribbon.

paper cachet

TYLER
by Maggie Holmes

Alphabet charms, jigsaw alphabets,
patterned cardstock, ribbon, rub-ons
mini, scrapbook colors acrylic paint
and staple: Making Memories
Game piece letter: Li'l Davis Designs
Metal stencil letter: Scrapworks
Other: Shadow box

how to: Print desired letter in a variety of sizes and fonts onto coordinating cardstock and cut
out. Paint Jigsaw Alphabet letter and separate. Separate another Jigsaw Alphabet letter, cover
with patterned cardstock and layer a coordinating cardstock behind the negative. Embellish
some of the letters with ribbon and mix with Alphabet Charms, metal stencil letter and game
piece letter. Arrange all letters in background of shadow box and adhere.

BIRTHDAY WISH
by Lilac Chang

Computer font: Modern No. 20

Crystal lacquer: Sakura Hobby Craft

Defined clear, eyelet letters, mini brads, page pebble, patterned cardstock, ribbon, scrapbook colors acrylic paint, shaped clip, tag and washer word: Making Memories

Metal bar: 7Gypsies

Numbers stamp: Danelle Johnson for Limited Edition

Transparency: Hewlett-Packard

how to: Create title using Custom Letters technique (see page 31) and attach down left side, overlapping pieces. Smear paint into Washer Word, wipe away excess and attach with a colored mini brad to dot the "i". Complete title with a combination of Page Pebbles backed with patterned cardstock and painted Eyelet Letters. Arrange and adhere to a square of cardstock and attach as a pocket. Create journaling block using Letters on Transparency technique (see page 31), add metal bar to top and slide behind pocket.

1. template

2. positive/negative

3. page pebble

4. transparency

by Lilac Chang

1. Use template to trace letters onto cardstock and cut out.

2. Print text in reverse onto cardstock and cut a square around letter. Bend in half
and cut away negative from top half and positive from bottom.

3. Place patterned cardstock behind a clear Page Pebble letter and trim away excess.

4. Print text onto transparency using white for text and black for background.
Attach to patterned cardstock with spray adhesive.

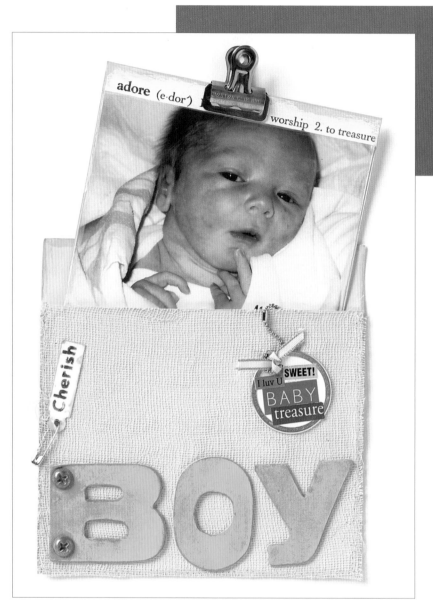

BOY
by Charla Campbell

Bead chain, cardstock tag, defined, jigsaw alphabets, latch card base and insert, magnetic stamps, scrapbook colors acrylic paint, snaps, stamping ink, tag and word fetti: Making Memories

Other: Cheesecloth, metal clip, ribbon and safety pin

how to: Trim latch from card base, adhere cheesecloth to front and stitch around edges of front flap to create a pocket. Attach photo and Defined sticker to insert and tuck inside. Paint Jigsaw Alphabet letters, lightly sand edges, attach screw snaps and adhere to front of card. Embellish with tags and metal clip.

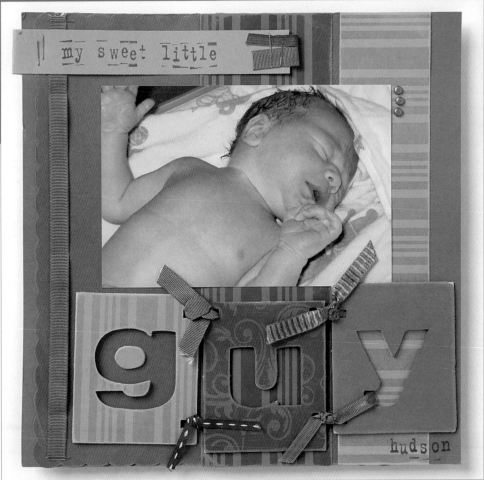

MY SWEET LITTLE GUY
by Robyn Werlich

Decorative-edged cardstock, jigsaw alphabets, magnetic stamps, mini brads, patterned cardstock, ribbon and staples: Making Memories
Stamping ink: Stampin' Up!

how to: Attach strips of patterned and scalloped cardstock to create striped background. Remove letters from Jigsaw Alphabets, cover negative pieces with cardstock and cut out openings with a craft knife. Sand all edges. Punch holes in top and bottom edges and tie together with various types of ribbon. Attach across bottom. Stamp remainder of title onto a strip of cardstock, rolling up and down to leave marks from edges of stamps.

HRW
by Robyn Werlich

Defined clear, fabric swatch, metal frame, moulding strip, patterned cardstock, ribbon, scrapbook colors acrylic paint and staples:
Making Memories

Letters: Quickutz

Other: Chipboard and denim

how to: Cut three chipboard rectangles in the same size and embellish as desired. Trace three large block initials onto patterned cardstock, cut out and attach to chipboard. Cut out letters from patterned cardstock and attach over block initials to spell names. Add embellishments. Turn all rectangles over, line up leaving ½ inch between each and attach together across the backs with four strips of ribbon.

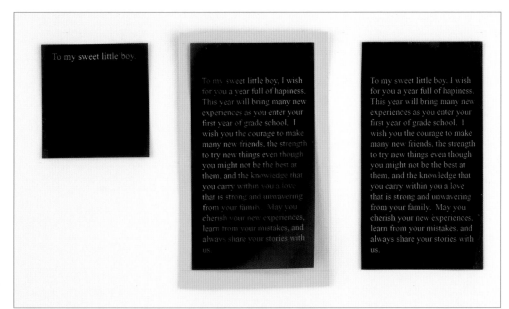

LETTERS ON TRANSPARENCY

1. Using word processing program, create a text box large enough to contain journaling block and fill with black or other background color.

2. Type text using white as foreground color.

3. Print onto transparency.

4. Back with colored or patterned cardstock, adhering with spray adhesive.

CUSTOM LETTERS

1. Print text in reverse onto cardstock using desired font and size.

2. Cut out letters using a craft knife.

3. Lay letters on waxed paper, apply thick coat of crystal lacquer or Diamond Glaze to each and let dry.

Being a little rough around the edges isn't always a bad thing. Tearing, rolling, scraping and roughening gives nearly anything dimension and calls attention to borders, pockets, backgrounds and more. Tear different types of paper to create one-of-a-kind accents or tear the middle from tags for unique mini frames. You'll get rugged and refined all at the same time.

TEARING

I Love You
by Charla Campbell

Alphabet stamps: Hero Arts
Cardstock tags, classic small
card base, decorative brads,
dyeable trims, photo anchors,
scrapbook colors acrylic paint and
stamping ink: Making Memories
Stamping ink: Colorbox
Other: Embroidery floss

paper cachet

how to: Cut flower petals and leaves from cardstock and sand edges. Peel layers of paper apart on edges of petals to create dimension. Rub ink over edges and dab paint randomly over surfaces. Arrange in a flower shape and attach together with painted Decorative Brad. Adhere to bottom right corner of card. Tear and roll bottom edge of card and edge with ink. Tear off edge from one of Cardstock Tags and ink.

Decorative-edged cardstock,
jigsaw alphabets, mini brads,
patterned cardstock and staples:
Making Memories

Other: Magnets and ribbon

how to: Cover positive and negative pieces of Jigsaw Alphabets letters with patterned cardstock using the Torn Paper and Decoupage Stencils technique (see page 41). Add strips of decorative-edged cardstock, mini brads, staples and ribbon to embellish. Roll edges, fold down corners and sand surfaces to distress. Adhere magnets on backs to complete.

WALKER RANCH PARK
by Erin Terrell

Brad and patterned cardstock:

Making Memories

Computer font: Incognitype

Walker Ranch Park
Daisy – Age 6 ½

how to: Cut several ¾-inch strips of patterned cardstock and tear one side to create ½-inch strips. Layer on top of patterned cardstock in the same color and pattern. Torn strips will create subtle background. Tear a thin strip and a wide strip along top edges and attach along bottom to create a border. Create an accent for journaling pocket by tearing and layering two flower shapes and tucking torn leaves under the petals.

1. scraping

2. rolled edge

3. flowers

4. border

by Erin Terrell

1. Tear edge of cardstock, scrape with edge scraper and attach as a pocket.

2. Tear the center out of a metal-rimmed tag, roll back and use to frame text or accent.

3. Tear long thin strips of cardstock, layer together to create a flower
and secure with a mini brad as center.

4. Tear and roll edges of several strips of cardstock in graduating widths to create border.

2 OF A KIND
by Joanna Bolick

Blossoms, foam stamps, like it is,
mailbox alphabet, mini brads,
patterned cardstock, rub-ons and
scrapbook colors acrylic paint:
Making Memories

Stamping ink: Nick Bantock

Other: Transparency

how to: Ink edges of background. Tear strips of patterned cardstock in coordinating colors and patterns and layer across page. Tear large corners from patterned cardstock and attach in top right and bottom left corners.

HI THERE
by Kim Hughes

Page pebble, patterned cardstock, ribbon, stitches, upright slot card base and insert, upright slot envelope and woven label: Making Memories

Ribbon: May Arts

Other: Stamping ink

how to: Tear patterned cardstock to create flower petals, leaves and grass. Arrange on front of card insert and envelope. Create stems with ribbon and braided Stitches. Create centers with Woven Label and Page Pebble backed with cardstock. Embellish pieces with ribbon.

TAYLOR'S ROOM
by Janet Hopkins

Alphabet charms, paper tags, patterned cardstock and
scrapbook colors acrylic paint: Making Memories
Cardboard door sign base: Michaels
Computer font: 2Peas Barefoot Professor
downloaded from www.twopeasinabucket.com
Ribbon: May Arts
Other: Bookplate, box, string and washers

how to: Tear 1-inch strips of patterned cardstock in
coordinating colors and wrap around cardboard
door sign base. Secure ends on the back. Wrap
ends in a gift-wrap style and staple with a staple
gun along top and bottom edges to secure. Punch
two holes through all layers at the top and string
ribbon through, knotting on the front. Add
further embellishments to complete.

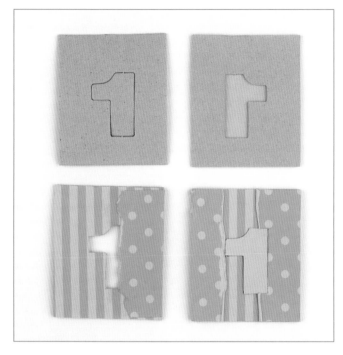

TORN PAPER AND DECOUPAGE STENCILS

1. Cut a piece of patterned cardstock to fit a stencil, such as a Jigsaw Alphabet letter or number. Remove inside, brush decoupage medium onto cardstock and adhere to stencil.

2. When dry, turn over and cut out number using a craft knife.

3. Tear a second piece of cardstock down the center and slightly roll back edges. Adhere with decoupage medium, leaving a space in between for first pattern to show through. Trim to fit, if necessary.

4. Turn over again and trim with a craft knife. Paint inside letter or number in a coordinating color and place back in opening.

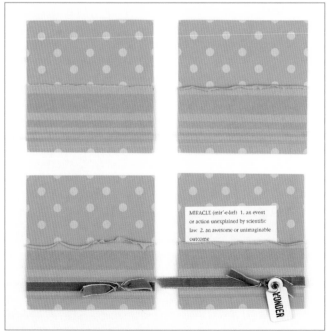

TORN AND ROLLED POCKET

1. Cut a strip of cardstock and tear the top edge.

2. Start rolling torn edge toward center of strip, making small tears if necessary.

3. Bend part of edge to make roll more pronounced. Attach on three sides to background to create pocket.

4. Tuck embellishment behind rolled edge pocket.

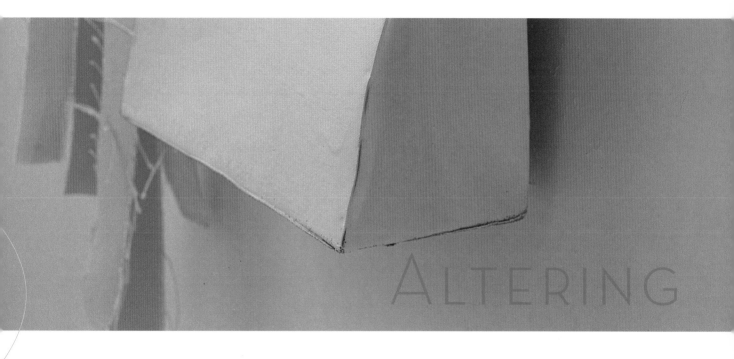

ALTERING

No matter how much you pinch, pull, suck in or slouch, sometimes, it just isn't going to fit. That's the time to call in the tailor. When your paper doesn't seem to work with your layout, card or craft, try a few alterations. Sand the surface and edges, perforate it with a sewing machine or cut it into strips and weave it together. A nip here, a tuck there and it'll be catwalk-ready in no time.

FRIENDSHIP
by Charla Campbell

Charmed, defined, dyeable trim, foam stamp, gatefold card base and insert and staples: Making Memories

Stamping ink: Colorbox

Other: Ribbon and shipping tags

how to: Crumple card base and iron to flatten. Scrape and ink edges of card and insert. Lightly stamp decorative image across top and bottom of front flaps with ink. Trim and tear Defined stickers, heavily ink edges and adhere to front and inside of card. Punch holes across top of insert and tie ribbon through. Add a length of trim across bottom of insert so that it is visible when card is closed.

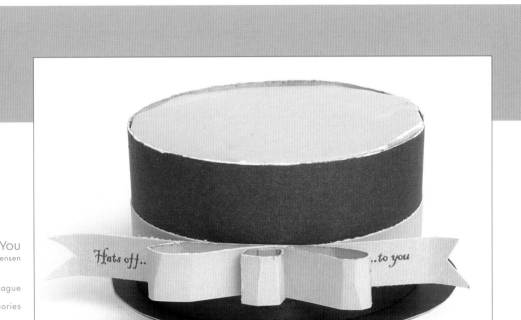

HATS OFF TO YOU
by Jennifer Jensen

Cosmo ribbon, hinge and league
paper: Making Memories

how to: Cut a 3½-inch circle for top of hat. Snip in ¼-inch around perimeter and fold snipped edges down. Cut a 1½ x 10½-inch strip for middle and attach ends together to create a circle. Glue snipped edges of circle to top edge of middle to create the top of the hat. Cut a ½ x 10½-inch strip of cardstock and wrap around to create ribbon. Add folded and clipped strips to complete bow. Cut another 3½-inch circle for the brim and attach hat to brim using a hinge. Print greeting on cardstock, fold, tie closed with ribbon and attach inside.

GRANDPA HOLMES
by Maggie Holmes

Alphabet stamps: PSX Design

Cardstock tags, distressing kit, jigsaw alphabet, jump rings, league paper, metal mesh, moulding corner, patterned cardstock, scrapbook colors acrylic paint, staples and word fetti: Making Memories

Ribbon: Li'l Davis Designs and Stampin' Up!

Stamping ink: StazOn by Tsukineko

Other: Jewelry tags, ribbon, safety pin and tulle

how to: Edge background with paint. Create six circles using the Sanding, Stitching and Perforating techniques (page 51) and attach in two rows on the left side of the page. Wrap several strips of ribbon around the right side of the photo and staple to secure. Place photo on metal mesh mat and staple to layout. Paint both pieces of Jigsaw Alphabet letter, sand outside edges and add Word Fetti stickers. Dangle from mesh with safety pin and jump rings.

1. metal mesh

2. foam stamp

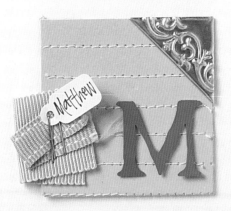

3. stitching

4. word fetti

by Maggie Holmes

1. Completely cover cardstock with metal mesh and staple on accents to attach.

2. Stamp cardstock with foam stamp and acrylic paint.

3. Straight stitch several lines horizontally across cardstock to add texture to background.

4. Completely cover cardstock background with Word Fetti or other stickers.

LimiTatiOnS, impossibilities, boundaries... little boys know no such rubbish.

little boys try everything you never thought of

SPENCER

your imagination knows **NO** bounds

SPENCER
by Erin Terrell

Distressing kit, league paper, like it is, metal mesh, mini brads, photo anchors and wooden tiles:
Making Memories

little boys try everything you never thought of

how to: Place a large piece of metal mesh behind background paper and, using a sanding block, sand front of paper so that pattern shows through. Move metal mesh around and continue sanding until entire background is altered.

1ST BIRTHDAY
by Maggie Holmes

Charmed photo corners, defined
clear, distressing kit, jigsaw
alphabet, league paper,
scrapbook colors acrylic paint
and tiny alphabets:
Making Memories
Ribbon: Li'l Davis Designs
Other: Board book,
jewelry tag and ribbon

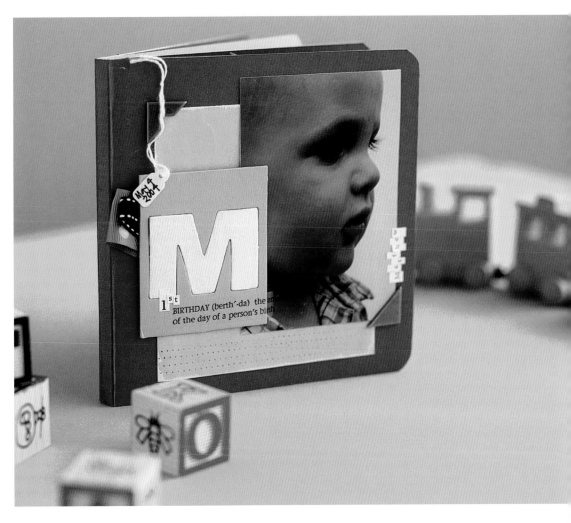

how to: Cover inside pages and covers of board book with solid sides of League paper. Create color blocks in coordinating colors of cardstock and use a variety of perforating, sanding, stitching and painting techniques to decorate. Attach photos and embellishments to create a custom storybook.

altering

FOREVER
by Kim Hughes

League paper, leather flowers, matchbook card base and insert, matchbook envelope, mini brads, ribbon, scrapbook colors acrylic paint and washer word: Making Memories

how to: Cut strips from League paper and adhere to front of card in a woven pattern. Cut piece of League paper to fit envelope and attach under flap. Embellish card and envelope with Leather Flowers, mini brads, a Washer Word and ribbon.

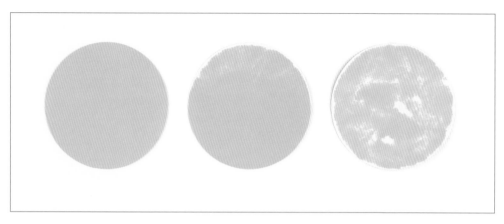

SANDING

1. Select cardstock background or cutout.

2. Use sandpaper or emery board from Distressing Kit and heavily sand edges, exposing the white core.

3. For a more aged look, sand entire surface, applying more pressure in certain areas to remove more of top layer.

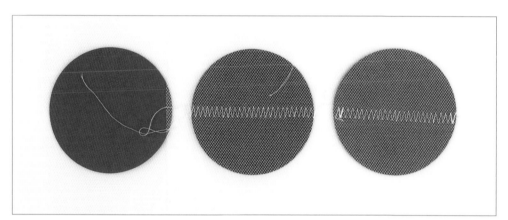

STITCHING

1. Select cardstock background or cutout. Cut a piece of tulle or sheer fabric that will completely cover it.

2. Layer fabric over cardstock and zigzag stitch together.

3. Trim excess fabric from edges.

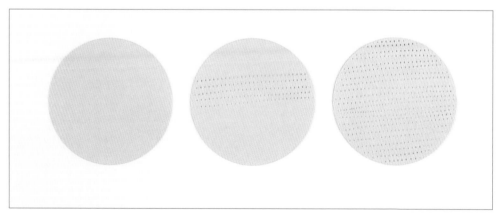

PERFORATING

1. Select cardstock background or cutout.

2. Using a sewing machine, zigzag stitch rows along paper with an unthreaded needle.

3. Continue stitching rows until piece is covered with holes.

CHAPTER

V

The French are known for their high style, impeccable taste and exceptional cuisine. So it's no wonder that they developed the fine art of decoupage. Go beyond the traditional practice of layering and adhering paper cutouts and experiment with flowers, ribbon, stickers, photos, cardboard and metal embellishments. You'll find that the results are trés chic!

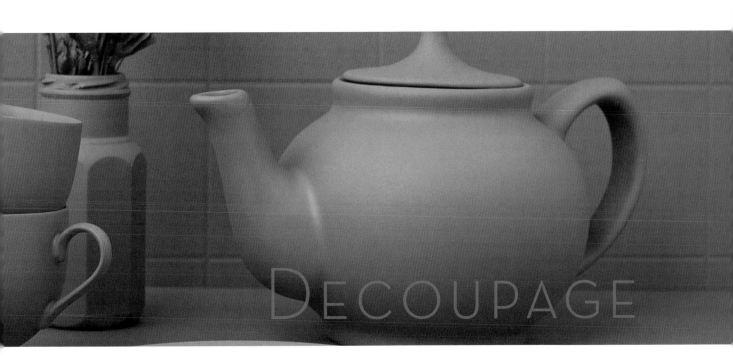

2 DECOUPAGE

M
by Maggie Holmes

Alpha fetti, alphabet rub-ons, blossoms, cosmopolitan embellishment paper, decorative brads, fashion paper, jigsaw alphabet, leather frame, ribbon, ribbon charm alphabets, ribbon charm letter wraps and scrapbook colors acrylic paint: Making Memories
Decoupage medium: Mod Podge by Plaid Enterprises
Monogram sticker: Diecuts with a View
Rub-on letters: Chatterbox
Stamping ink: Ranger Industries
Other: Chipboard, game piece, jewelry tag, rhinestones, ribbon and silk flower

how to: Trim several blocks of patterned and solid cardstock in various sizes, arrange and adhere to chipboard background. Brush decoupage medium over entire surface and let dry. Apply rub-ons over decoupaged areas and complete layout with photo and a variety of embellishments.

CIGAR BOX PURSE
by Janet Hopkins

Blossoms, cosmopolitan embellishment paper, ribbon and scrapbook colors acrylic paint: Making Memories Brackets, purse handle and wood cigar box: Darice Other: Charm and decoupage medium

how to: Paint edges of box. Trace front and back of box onto Cosmopolitan paper and cut out. Lightly sand and paint edges and stitch around outside edges and along seams. Layer Blossoms where patterns intersect on front panel and wrap ribbon around, dangling charm from knot. Decoupage finished covers to front and back of box and add hardware.

LOVE
by Maggie Holmes

Charmed, charmed words, dyeable
trim, eyelets, jump rings, metal
mesh, moulding strips, patterned
cardstock, ribbon and scrapbook
colors acrylic paint: Making Memories
Decoupage medium: Mod Podge
by Plaid Enterprises
Paper: SEI
Stickers: Diecuts with a View
Other: Corrugated cardboard
and ribbon

how to: Cut cardboard to desired size and create background using Cardboard Background
technique (see page 61). Set eyelets in each corner of photos and hang from metal mesh with
jump rings. Cut two Moulding Strips to fit along right and bottom edges, mitering corners.
Before applying strip onto right edge, tie ribbon and rickrack around top half. Add journaling
to small rectangle and tuck behind photo.

1. metal

2. stickers

3. blossoms

4. metal mesh

by Maggie Holmes

1. Apply stickers to metal background and brush decoupage medium over surface.

2. Adhere Alpha Fetti stickers to a Jigsaw Alphabet or stencil letter and decoupage surface.

3. Decoupage paper products onto cardstock such as Blossoms flowers.

4. Decoupage metal embellishments such as metal mesh, metal-rimmed tags and Petite Signage.

SWEET
by Joy Bohan

Decoupage medium: Mod Podge
by Plaid Enterprises
Fabric pocket, gatefold card base,
gatefold envelope, magnetic stamps,
metal word, ribbon, safety pin and
scrapbook colors acrylic paint:
Making Memories
Stamping ink: Vivid by Clearsnap
Other: Dowel

how to: Cut thin dowel rods
to desired size and paint. Cut
¼-inch strips of cardstock in
a contrasting color, brush
both sides generously with
decoupage medium and wind
around painted rods in a spiral
pattern. When dry, tie together
with ribbon and tuck into
pocket on front of card.

J
by Jennifer Jensen

Cosmopolitan embellishment paper,
foam stamp and scrapbook colors
acrylic paint: Making Memories
Decoupage medium: Mod Podge
by Plaid Enterprises
Other: Buttons, cardboard
and rhinestones

how to: Trace or draw front and back of letter onto cardboard. Wrap and adhere thin strips of Cosmopolitan paper around each piece until covered. Heavily coat both pieces with decoupage medium and set aside to dry. While front piece is still tacky, stamp images with paint and add centers. Cut two strips of 2x12-inch Cosmopolitan paper and fold in long edges ½ inch. Glue together to form one long strip and glue down folded edges. Hot glue front of letter to top edge of strip, working in small sections. When strip is completely wrapped around letter, glue back piece to opposite edge of strip. Heavily decoupage front, sides and back to secure pieces together.

decoupage

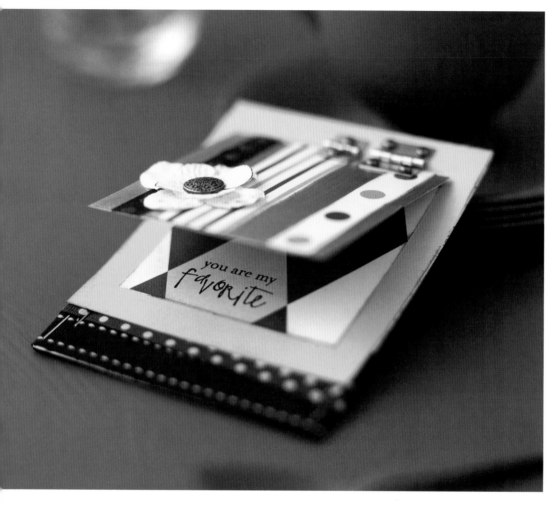

YOU ARE MY FAVORITE
by Maggie Holmes

Blossoms, cosmopolitan embellishment
paper, decorative brad, hinges, metal
sheet, mini brads, ribbon, rub-ons,
staples and upright slot card base:
Making Memories

Decoupage medium: Mod Podge
by Plaid Enterprises

Stamping ink: Ranger Industries

Other: Ribbon

how to: Cut a square from metal sheet to fit front of card. Trim strips of Cosmopolitan paper
and ribbon, ink with stamp pad and attach to metal square. Brush decoupage medium over
front and back surfaces and add layered Blossoms attached with Decorative Brad to bottom
corner. Use hinges to create a flap with embellished metal piece. Inside of card is under flap.

CARDBOARD BACKGROUND

1. Cut a piece of corrugated cardboard to desired size.

2. Tear off top layer to expose some corrugations.

3. Use a foam brush to apply acrylic paint to surface.

4. Apply decoupage medium to backs of ribbon and cardstock and adhere to cardboard in desired pattern.

5. Brush decoupage medium over entire surface of cardboard, allow to dry for 15 minutes and apply a second coat.

6. Embellish as desired.

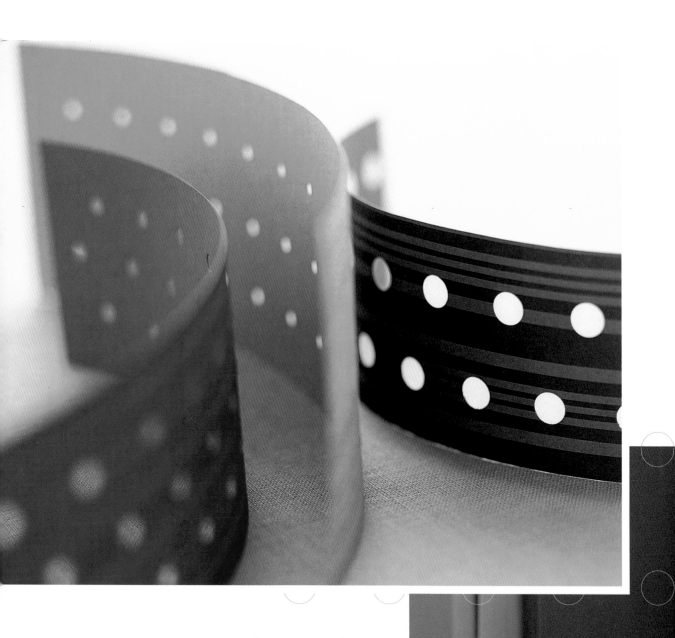

Herbal supplements, bikram yoga and organic everything. Holistic lifestyles have gone mainstream. Why not take a hole-istic approach to punching too? Circles are calming, serene and orderly and you'll be amazed at what you can do with them. Use them alone or combine them with other punched shapes to create graphic patterns and designs that are simple or intricate but always stunning. They'll make you oooo, ahhh and ohhh.

PUNCHING

NIGHTLIGHT
By Janet Hopkins

Brads, distressing kit, patterned
cardstock, scrapbook colors
acrylic paint and safety pin:
Making Memories

Self-adhesive nightlight shade: Michaels

Ribbon: May Arts

Other: Punches

how to: Trace template in nightlight shade packaging onto patterned cardstock. Cut out and attach. Punch several flowers in various sizes and shapes from coordinating colors of patterned cardstock. Sand and dry brush punched shapes to distress. Stitch a row of flowers together and attach across top of shade. Layer shapes together, embellish with brads, ribbon and a safety pin and attach across bottom edge of shade.

FRIENDSHIP
by Janet Hopkins

Computer fonts: Civilian and McGarey
downloaded from the Internet

Decorative brads, gatefold card, base and insert,
patterned cardstock and scrapbook colors
acrylic paint: Making Memories

Punch: EK Success

Transparency: 3M

Other: Punch

how to: Print text onto transparency, cut to fit front of card and slit down the middle to fit front flaps. Punch one small and three large flowers from patterned cardstock to create each flower for front. Crumple, distress with ink and paint the edges of each piece. Stack together, attaching with a Decorative Brad and adhere to front flaps so that petals intertwine when card is closed. Attach a small punched flower to top edge of insert to act as a pull tab.

a father's advice to his son

approaching manhood

johnathan

balance

open

A FATHER'S ADVICE
by Julie Turner

Computer font: Verdana
by WordPerfect
Eyelet charm tag, label holder,
mailbox alphabet, mini brads,
patterned cardstock, petite
signage and snap:
Making Memories
Punches: Marvy Uchida
Other: Envelope

how to: Cut three strips of patterned cardstock to fully cover background piece of cardstock. Punch a vertical line of 1/8-inch holes down the middle strip and back holes with cardstock in a contrasting color. Punch a horizontal line of 3/16-inch holes in the right strip, back with a contrasting color and plug one of the holes. Attach all strips to the background and round corners. Punch a half circle in upper left side and attach a piece of contrasting cardstock behind to create a pocket. Slide Eyelet Charm Tag inside.

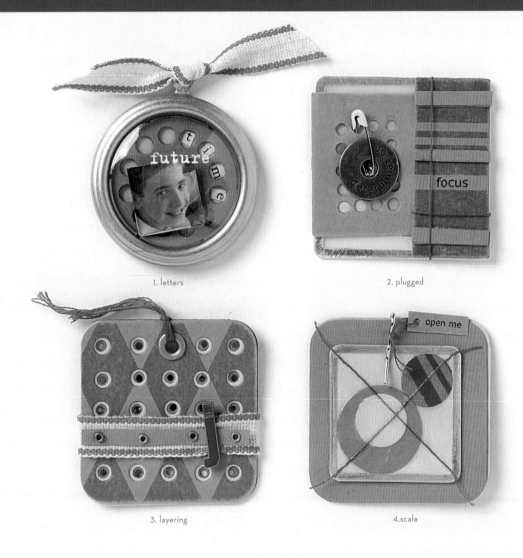

1. letters

2. plugged

3. layering

4. scale

by Julie Turner

1. Place Tiny Alphabets letters under punched circles to spell word.

2. Hang embellishments from a punched and plugged background.

3. Create background using Layered Designs technique (see page 71).

4. Layer different sizes and patterns of punched circles to create an accent.

SEAMUS
by Lisa McGarvey

Cardstock tag, leather flower,
mini brad and patterned
cardstock: Making Memories

Paper: Bazzill Basics

Punches: EK Success
and Marvy Uchida

how to: Round corners with punch on opposite corners of background blocks. Punch circles in various sizes from patterned and textured cardstocks. Punch smaller circles out of larger ones and arrange all shapes to create border along right edge of layout. Add punched flower shapes to finish the design.

how to: Punch circles from cardstock using a 1-inch circle punch. Punch a variety of shapes from cardstock in coordinating colors. Edge all pieces with ink, adhere shapes inside circles and add mini brads. Use embellished circles to decorate invitations, place cards, favor bags and more.

SUMMER PARTY ENSEMBLE
by Wendy Anderson

Alphabet rub-ons, decorative-edged cardstock, mini brads and patterned cardstock: Making Memories

Punches: EK Success and McGill

Stamping ink: Stewart Superior Corp.

CIRCLE OF LIFE
by Joy Bohan

Computer fonts: Century
Schoolbook and Modern No. 20
downloaded from the Internet

Latch card base, latch envelope,
patterned cardstock and ribbon
charm: Making Memories

Stamping ink: Memories
by Stampcraft

Other: Corner rounder
and punches

In the full circle of life there are good days and bad

how to: Punch circles in two shapes from a variety of colors
and patterns of patterned cardstock. Arrange circles in a
random pattern to line right and bottom edges of card front.
Round corners of card with a corner rounder and add circles
along inside edge of card to create a tab effect.

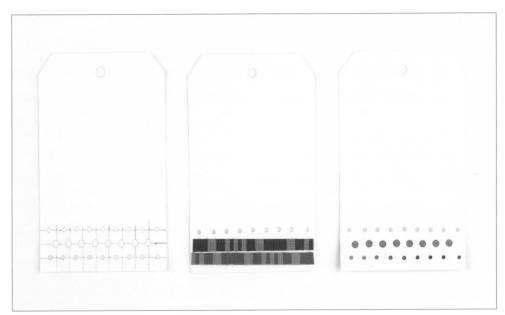

PUNCHED DESIGNS

1. Lightly pencil desired pattern onto cardstock and punch with various sizes of punches.

2. Back the holes with contrasting strips of cardstock.

3. From the front, holes will be filled in with color.

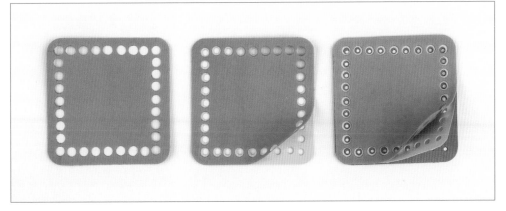

LAYERED DESIGNS

1. Select three contrasting colors of cardstock and cut to same size.

2. Punch 3/16-inch holes in desired pattern on top piece.

3. Back with second color and punch 1/8-inch holes through first holes.

4. Back with third color and punch 1/16-inch holes through first and second holes.

STAMPING WITH BLEACH

Whether we like it or not, we're all creatures of habit. But, every once in a while, it sure feels good to bust out of that routine. Here's the perfect chance. Set aside your stamp pads and use bleach as your stamping ink instead. Better yet, dip household items, metal embellishments or anything else with a flat surface into bleach and stamp away. It's a little daring, a little crazy and a lot of fun.

HOLMES 2004
by Maggie Holmes

Blossoms, defined, dyeable trims, eyelet charms, eyelet letters, foam stamps, ledger paper, metal frame, patterned cardstock, ribbon charm letter wraps, scrapbook dye and staples: Making Memories

Concho: Scrapworks

Printed twill tape: 7Gypsies

Stamps: B Line Designs and Inkadinkado

Tin set: Provo Craft

Other: Bleach, paper clips and ribbon

how to: Use foam stamps and bleach to stamp images onto cardstock. Trim into strips or cut into circles to decorate the outside cover and inside of tin box and canisters.

CALL ME
by Jayme Shepherd

Avenue embellishment paper, distressing kit, dyeable trim,
foam stamps, ribbon, upright slot card base and insert and
woven label: Making Memories
Other: Bleach

how to: Dip foam stamps into bleach and stamp onto
insert. Trim ½ inch from top and side of insert and
cut mat from Avenue paper. Ink edges and attach. Ink
edges of base and slide insert through slot. Tie trim and
ribbon over slot and add woven label.

Precious Time
By Loni Stevens

Computer fonts: 2Peas
Weathervane downloaded from
www.twopeasinabucket.com and
Bell MT by Microsoft Word

Defined clear, eyelets, jump rings,
label holder, petite signage, ribbon
and snap: Making Memories

Clock stamp: Stampers Anonymous

Elastic: 7Gypsies

Transparency: Hammermill

Other: Bleach corner punch,
foam core and silk flower

how to: Brush bleach onto clock stamp, blot and stamp onto cardstock. Attach silk flower to center of image. Dip the end of a stylus into bleach and stamp a dotted border around the clock. Cut opening from cardstock and foam core. Set eyelets in each corner of photo and suspend by looping jump rings through eyelets and through eye pins pushed into foam core. Attach printed transparency on the back of cardstock and mount to foam core background. Adhere cardstock backing to back of foam core and trim to fit.

1. jar lid

2. rubber stamp

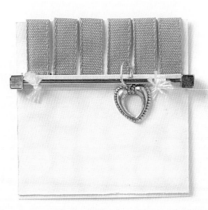

3. pencil eraser

4. foam stamp

by Loni Stevens

1. Use a metal jar lid as a stamp, overlapping images to create a graphic background.

2. Using bleach as stamping ink, stamp image with rubber stamp.

3. Dip pencil eraser into bleach and stamp over cardstock in a random pattern.

4. Create border with bleach and stamp , then stamp text over the top with black ink.

we'll **ALWAYS** be family, no matter what

cole &
daddy   *summer '03*

COLE & DADDY
by Joanna Bolick

Avenue embellishment paper, blossoms, foam stamp, like it is, mini brad and patterned cardstock: Making Memories
Computer fonts: Baskerville Regular and Italic by Mac OS X
Other: Bleach, buttons, transparency and waxed linen

how to: Dip foam stamp into bleach and stamp several rows across cardstock. Trim to fit background. Print title onto transparency, trim to same size as stamped cardstock and attach. Add photo, sticker and embellishments to finish.

HELLO
by Jayme Shepherd

Avenue embellishment paper, charmed frame, foam stamp, jelly label,
MM kids trim and upright window card base: Making Memories
Other: bleach

how to: Dab foam stamp onto bleach-soaked paper towel and
stamp randomly on front of card. Cut flowers from trim and
attach as centers. Place square of Avenue paper, Charmed
Frame and Jelly Label in opening.

STATIONERY SET
by Jennifer Jensen

Avenue embellishment paper, foam stamp,
ribbon and tag: Making Memories
Other: Bleach, button, chipboard, magazine
letters, pipe cleaner, ribbon and tulle

how to: : Cut chipboard to 10¾ x 11¼ inches and fold to create a book
cover with a ½-inch spine. Cover inside and outside with paper. Stitch
cardstock together to create pockets for inside and fill with stationery and
envelopes. Use foam stamp and bleach to stamp flower image onto two
colors of cardstock and cut out. Layer together with tulle, add a button
for the center and adhere to front cover. Further embellish with tag,
fibers and ribbon.

UNEXPECTED ITEMS AS STAMPS

1. Turn any items with a flat surface into a stamp, such as jar lids, pencil erasers, metal embellishments, etc.

2. Dip item into bleach, soaking for as long as necessary and place onto item to be stamped.

2. Experiment with pattern, overlapping, random stamping or lining up images.

stamping with bleach

Military uniforms stand out in a crowd. Maybe it's the perfectly pressed fabric or the crisp creases in just the right places. They're tailored, precise and clean. Artful folding of paper can have the same effect. Folded patterns and decorative pleats are beautiful on their own. But even better when enhanced with dye or chalk. Whatever technique you choose, your designs will command attention.

FOLDING

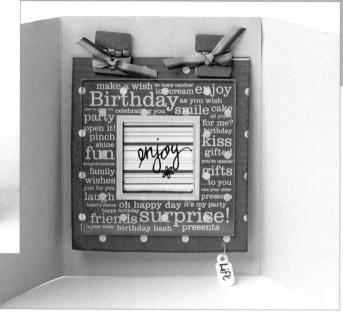

HAPPY BIRTHDAY
by Kara Wylie

Cosmo ribbon, cosmopolitan
embellishment paper, hinges, jump
ring, mailbox alphabet, rub-ons mini
and sheer frame: Making Memories

Other: Jewelry tag and
paper crimper

how to: Create a tri-fold card out of cardstock. Trim a square of Cosmopolitan paper to fit
front flap, run through paper crimper, fold ends forward and stitch. Add embellishment and
rub-on to complete front. Crimp a second square of Cosmopolitan paper, attach Sheer Frame
to top and use hinges to create flap on inside of card. Create mini tri-fold to place underneath.

SOFT & SWEET
by Lisa McGarvey

Alphabet charm, cardstock tag, cosmopolitan embellishment paper, eyelet letter, eyelet tag alphabet, mini brad, petite signage, ribbon, stitches and woven label: Making Memories

Clock face: Manto Fe

Metal clasp: Scrapworks

Tags: Avery

Other: Envelope, molded paper, quilting pin, ribbon and woven paper

how to: Create a folded pocket border by using a metal ruler to score and fold a strip of cardstock at 1-inch intervals. Measure ¼ inch up from each fold and score and fold again. Fold strip together in a random accordion-style fashion, securing with a pin, stitching, twine and a metal clasp. Adhere strip to page and tuck various accents into folds.

folding

BEACH MEMORIES
by Julie Turner

Cardstock, cosmopolitan embellishment
paper, mini brad and scrapbook dye:
Making Memories

Computer fonts: Bernhard
Modern and Times New Roman
by Microsoft Word

Photo corner: 7Gypsies

Other: Transparency

I love to let the really big waves crash over me. Sometimes they lift me up and carry me to the shore. Way cool! — Jackson, 2004

la jolla beach *memories*

how to: Cut background cardstock ¾ inch wider than desired when finished. Print title along right edge and fold several creases and one box pleat on left side. Side folds of box pleat should measure ⅜ inch each and width of background should now measure as desired. Add color using Highlighting Folds technique with dye (see page 91). Cut Cosmopolitan paper to fit the right side of the layout and attach, tucking under right side of pleat. Cut a slit into right edge of paper and fold back to reveal printed title.

1. box pleats

2. rolled creases

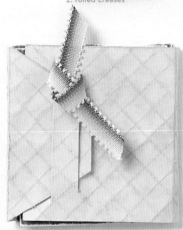

3. fanned folds

4. diamond folds

by Julie Turner

1. Print onto cardstock and create a series of box pleats, folding so that text is visible. Use strip to create a pocket.

2. Cut two horizontal slits into cardstock, slit down middle and roll each side back by creating a series of creases on the flaps.

3. Cut a corner out of cardstock and fold in a fanned design. Fold back top edge.

4. Fold cover of a mini book on both diagonals at equal distances to create a diamond pattern. Dye to highlight creases.

how to: Cut cardboard backing to 12x12 inches. Cut 12 strips of 3x12-inch Cosmopolitan paper in a variety of patterns and solids. Score 1 inch from the bottom of each strip and fold to the back to create a small pocket. Stitch along top of 2-inch strip sides and adhere the 1-inch strip sides to the backing, overlapping strips until cardboard is covered. Wrap Fabric Tape vertically along right and left sides to hold strips down. Staple ribbon on top, tie rings along top edge and attach bead chain through for hanging. Tuck cards or other memorabilia between strips.

MEMENTOS
by Janet Hopkins

Chain and rings: Home Depot

Computer font: 1946 downloaded from the Internet

Cosmo ribbon, cosmopolitan embellishment paper, fabric tape, label holder,

mailbox alphabet, rub-ons, scrapbook colors acrylic paint,

staples and washer word: Making Memories

Other: Cardboard and ribbon

how to: Create several vertical folds across Mini Book cover and apply walnut ink with a foam brush to highlight creases. Let dry. Cut a rectangle of Cosmopolitan paper, fold over top and bottom edges and stitch together. Add embellishments and attach to front cover. Insert inner pages and complete book.

ERNEST BRADBURY HANSEN
by Hillary Bevan

Alphabet charms, cosmo ribbon, cosmopolitan embellishment paper, ledger paper,

mini book cover, mini book inner pages, ribbon charm and shaped clip: Making Memories

Other: Walnut ink

DAD
by Kim Hughes

Alphabet charms, cosmopolitan embellishment paper, foam stamps, hinge, mini brad, photo anchor, ribbon, scrapbook colors acrylic paint, tag with pocket card base and insert and tag with pocket envelope: Making Memories

Other: Stamp

how to: Accordion-fold a strip of Cosmopolitan paper several times to create a rectangular mini book. Fold up bottom edge to create pockets on each page. Wrap hinge and ribbon around left edge to create binding and attach to front of card base. Attach photo anchor with mini brad on right edge to hold book closed.

FOLDING

1. Fold pattern into cardstock, creasing each fold with a bone folder.

2. Experiment to create stripes, squares, diamonds or random patterns.

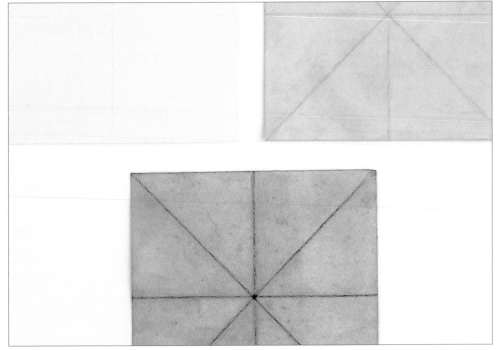

HIGHLIGHTING FOLDS

1. Dip folded cardstock into dye to accentuate creases. The dye will absorb darker in creased areas.

2. Use a cotton swab to rub chalk over creases to highlight.

CHAPTER

IX

Hire an interior designer and she'll tell you a room isn't complete without accessories. Books, candles, wall hangings—they're the personal touches that make a house a home. Decorate your pages and projects with custom, handmade embellishments. Creating them from paper is quick, easy and guarantees a perfect match every time. They'll take your pages from unfinished to unbelievable.

EMBELLISHMENTS

How Do You
by Maggie Holmes

League paper, ribbon, scrapbook
colors acrylic paint and staples:
Making Memories

Other: Ribbon, tulle and twill tape

how to: Freehand cut several flower shapes from the solid side of League paper. Straight stitch around petals using a sewing machine. Layer flowers together on wall hanging, gather three squares of tulle in the center and hand stitch around the middle to secure, tying off on the back of the piece.

HEY
by Kim Hughes

Computer font: Saginaw

Gatefold card base and insert,

jelly label and league paper:

Making Memories

Punches: EK Success

Stamping ink: Ink-Crafter's Pigment Ink

how to: Tear along gatefold to create rough edges. Cut two strips of League paper, ink edges and adhere to front of card. Create flower from League paper and punches, layer and attach to left strip. Add jelly label to right strip and print greeting onto insert.

embellishments

SIMPLE BEAUTY
by Julie Turner

Computer font: Georgia
by WordPerfect

League paper and word fetti:
Making Memories

Ribbon: Bucilla

Other: Decorative scissors,
florist wire and plastic clip

how to: Trim cardstock strips in various widths with pinking scissors, sand edges and layer to create a decorative background. Add a thin cardstock strip vertically down left side. Create two flowers using the Shaped Flowers technique (see page 101) and tie to strip with ribbon.

1. punch shapes

2. dangling

3. pocket

4. accent with paint

by Julie Turner

1. Layer two punched shapes and line along edge of background to create a border.

2. Slide paper embellishments onto a stick pin and use to dangle a tag or create a closure.

3. Glue a cardstock embellishment to end of paper clip and slide onto edge of pocket.

4. Add detail to cardstock accents with paint. Cut slits into background and slide embellishment through to hold in place.

Hi
by Wendy Anderson

Avenue embellishment paper, classic small card base, gameboard shape,
jigsaw alphabets, league paper and scrapbook colors acrylic paint:
Making Memories
Ribbon: Offray

how to: Trim League paper to fit front of card and edge with
paint. Paint Jigsaw Alphabet letters and attach to right side.
Cut strip of Avenue paper and attach across middle of card,
adding Gameboard Shape flower to embellish.

ENJOY
by Robyn Werlich

Decorative scissors: Fiskars

Brad, foam stamp, league paper,

mini brads, photo anchor, rub-ons

mini, scrapbook colors acrylic paint

and staples: Making Memories

Ribbon: Stampin' Up!

Other: Punches, ribbon

and transparency

how to: Fold League paper to create a bag. Use a small gift bag as a template, if necessary. Before attaching, cut an opening out of front, stitch transparency into window, stamp letter and apply rub-on. Punch several flower shapes, cut strips of paper with decorative scissors and attach around window. Fold bag. Punch holes along seam, thread ribbon through and tie closed. Fill with candy or gift, punch two holes along top edge and tie closed with ribbon.

FASHION CHALLENGED
by Erin Terrell

Alphabet rub-ons, league paper,

mini brads and word fetti:

Making Memories

Computer font:

2Peas Sailboat downloaded from

www.twopeasinabucket.com

Label maker: DYMO

Punch: EK Success

Rub-on letters: Rusty Pickle

Stamping ink: Memories by

Stampcraft

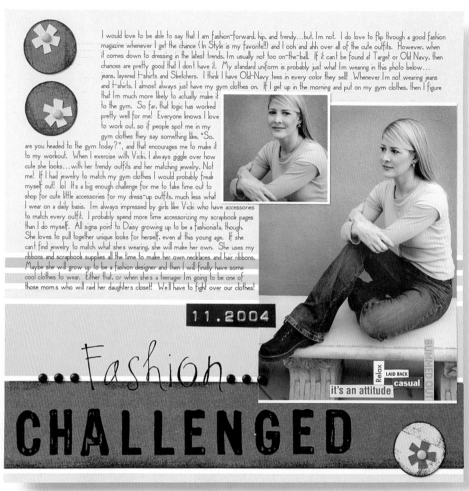

how to: Punch or cut circles from cardstock and rub ink pad over edges and surfaces. Punch flower or other shapes from contrasting colors of cardstock and attach off-center to circles using mini brads. Place circles along edges of layout to embellish.

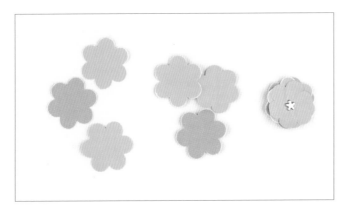

LAYERED FLOWERS

1. Punch three flowers in coordinating colors and trim the petals down on the one that will be the top layer.

2. Lightly sand edges and crumple to give flowers dimension and subtle texture.

3. Layer and attach together with a brad.

4. Experiment with different materials for the layers, such as patterned paper, fabric or tulle. Paint or dye layers and use unique buttons or fasteners for centers.

FOLDED FLOWERS

1. Punch a circle from cardstock.

2. Fold four times so piece resembles a pie cut into eighths. Pinch a tiny fold next to each crease to give flower a raised appearance. Lightly sand edges and folds.

3. Add a brad as center, wire as stem and tied ribbon strip as leaves.

SHAPED FLOWERS

1. Punch three hearts from cardstock.

2. Shape into petals by creasing down the middle and rolling the ends around the handle of a small paintbrush.

3. Join petals together with liquid glue, lightly pinching at the base until glue dries and sets.

4. When dry, pierce a small hole in center. Create a tiny loop at the end of a wire and run through so that the loop is the center. Anchor with a tiny dab of glue and add ribbon and decorative beads, if desired.

PAPER QUILTING

Imagine a room full of women sitting around a cozy fire. They've got needles, thread and thimbles and they're piecing, tying and stitching. This isn't a quilting bee. It's a scrapbooking night. You can participate in the time-honored, nostalgic hobby of quilting without ever touching a scrap of fabric. Try these techniques and, just like a handmade quilt, you'll wrap your pages and projects in warmth and love.

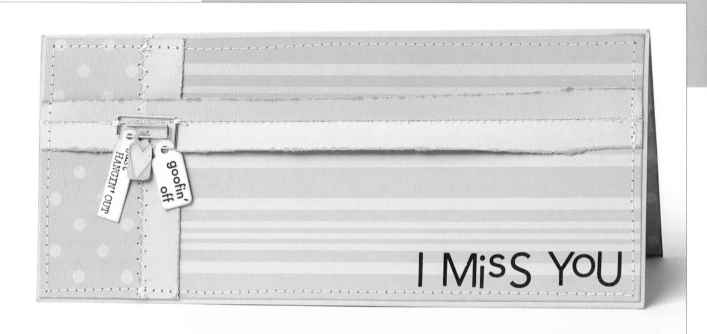

I Miss You
by Wendy Anderson

Alphabet rub-ons, cardstock tags, patterned cardstock, shaped clip and upright window card base and insert: Making Memories

Stamping ink: Stewart Superior Corp.

Tag: Doodlebug Designs

how to: With back sides together, straight stitch two strips of patterned cardstock together leaving a 1-inch seam allowance. Tear to remove ½ inch from seam allowance, leaving an uneven edge. Open pieces and fold seam open. Cut a rectangle of cardstock in a coordinating color and pattern, fold right side over, cut into two pieces and slide under seam openings, lining up left edges. Zigzag stitch along folded over seam to secure. Trim piece to fit front of card and straight stitch around all edges. Add shaped clip, tags and rub-ons.

PICTURE FRAME
by Jayme Shepherd

Avenue embellishment paper,
decorative-edged cardstock,
MM kids trim, patterned cardstock,
ribbon and woven ribbon:
Making Memories

Other: 4x6 photo frame

how to: Trim cardstock to fit front of frame and cut out center opening with craft knife. Cut several strips of patterned cardstock and Avenue Paper and stitch onto paper frame. Tie strips of ribbon around edge. Trim decorative-edged cardstock to create border around stitched piece, attach together and adhere to front of frame.

THE SWING
by Julie Turner

Patterned cardstock and snap:

Making Memories

HOW DO YOU   LIKE TO GO UP IN A SWING,   UP IN THE AIR SO HIGH?
OH, I DO THINK IT THE PLEASANTEST THING   EVER A CHILD CAN DO!

JILLIAN 10/04

how to: Layer several pieces of patterned cardstock in various coordinating colors, sizes and patterns to create a crazy-quilt look. Adhere to cardstock backing and zigzag stitch all seams together. Before stitching top layers, slide photo underneath and then stitch. Attach small accent photo and straight stitch down left and right sides. Add journaling and heart snap.

JILLIAN 10/04

1. hand-tied quilt

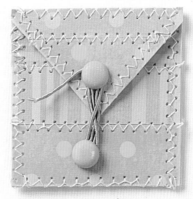

2. crazy quilt

3. open seams

4. pieced quilt

by Julie Turner

1. Cut small squares, fold diagonally to give them dimension and arrange in rows.
Tie through with Stitches to create look of a hand-tied quilt.

2. Zigzag stitch several pieces of cardstock together to make a crazy-quilt pocket.

3. Sew several pieces of cardstock together and place photos or
embellishments in the windows created by seam openings.

4. Stitch squares and rectangles together and attach snaps
or other embellishments in individual pieces.

JOY
by Robyn Werlich

Defined clear, eyelet tag alphabet,
mini brads, patterned cardstock, ribbon
and staples: Making Memories

Other: Ribbon

how to: Cut diamond shapes in the same size from three coordinating patterned or solid cardstocks. Adhere first row across bottom of layout so that side points touch. Stitch around edges of top layer of diamonds and adhere over first row. Stitch through both layers of diamonds using a contrasting thread to create an argyle-patterned border.

how to: Cut cardstock backing to fit the cover of a CD case. Cut or punch several 1¾-inch squares from patterned and solid cardstock. Trim some edges with decorative scissors, layer on backing and attach. Stitch diagonally at 1-inch intervals. Add mini brads and beads along stitching lines, add further embellishments and attach backing to case.

FOREVER FRIENDS
by Jennifer Jensen

Decorative scissors: Fiskars

Eyelet charm tag, mini brads, patterned cardstock and woven label: Making Memories

Other: CD case, flower, flower beads, ribbon and string

MIRACLE
by Maggie Holmes

Classic small card base, patterned
cardstock, rub-ons mini, staple and
stitched tin tile: Making Memories
Sticker: Pebbles Inc.
Other: Ribbon

how to: **Cut a piece of cardstock
backing to the same size as
the front of the card. Trim
several rectangles and squares
from patterned cardstock,
arrange to completely cover
backing and trim edges to fit.
Use a sewing machine to
straight stitch around outside
edge and a variety of zigzag
stitches to stitch along all
seams. Attach piece over
front flap of card and
embellish as desired.**

PIECED QUILT

1. Cut several squares and rectangles of cardstock.

2. With right sides together, stitch pieces to create a pieced quilt look.

3. Press open seams by folding back and creasing.

LAYOUT GALLERY

DREAM
by Loni Stevens

Blossom, cardstock, decorative brad,
eyelet, mini brad, cardstock tag and
photo anchor: Making Memories

Paper: Pebbles Inc.

Twill tape: Scenic Route

how to: Lightly trace a grid onto cardstock with a pencil and straight edge and punch holes where lines intersect. Erase lines, turn piece over and back with squares of cardstock in various colors. Use same technique in a circular pattern in corner of photo.

HAPPY
by Loni Stevens

Blossom, eyelets, jigsaw
alphabets, patterned cardstock,
petite signage, scrapbook
colors acrylic paint and snap:
Making Memories
Computer font: Courier
by Microsoft Word
Corner rounder: Creative Memories
Elastic: 7Gypsies
Other: Ribbon

My older sister Jodi's wedding reception was held at
our Chapman cousins' home in Provo where the landscape
includes a large pond in the front of their beautiful
home. My niece Tyra quickly changed out of her dress
during the reception and was joined on the pond by Josh
and Austin. They each took turns rowing the boat and
gliding sticks along the top of the water as the other
rowed. I captured this moment between the three
cousins as Josh was giggling over something silly.
Go figure. That's Josh for you! Always smiling. 5.20.00

how to: Cut six squares of patterned cardstock, score along edges where paper meets and fold
up. Layer in groups of two, arrange along left edge of background, butting squares up to each
other and attach. Secure by double stitching around the inside of each square. Tear away
corners and along folded up edges and bend and roll down. Paint Jigsaw Alphabet letters and
attach inside squares to create title.

SISTER-IN-LAW & FRIEND
by Maggie Holmes

Alphabet charms, artisan labels, blossom, cardstock, decorative brads, foam stamps, label holders, leather flowers, leather frame, mini brads and ribbon: Making Memories

Bleach: Clorox

Foam stamp: Li'l Davis Designs

Rubber stamps: B Line Designs and Postmodern Design

Stamping ink: Ranger Industries

Other: Jewelry tags and ribbon

how to: Cut squares to cover background, arrange and edge with ink. Brush bleach onto various stamps and stamp images onto squares. Attach squares to background and zigzag stitch around edges. Mix Alphabet Charms with stamped letters to complete names, and add further embellishments as desired.

SOPHIA
by Loni Stevens

Computer font: Courier
by Microsoft Word

Corner rounder: Creative Memories

Defined clear, eyelet charms, label
holder, league paper, magnetic date
stamp, mini brads and photo anchors:
Making Memories

Embossing template: Fiskars

Other: Chipboard

how to: Round corners of background piece of League paper. Mat photos and print title on cardstock. Use Eyelet Charm flower to emboss image above text and trim to size. Position on page and cut an embossing template out of chipboard slightly larger than photo and text block. Emboss rectangle along top of background and attach pieces inside. Score across a rectangular piece of cardstock and fold so that back edge is slightly higher than front. Place front flap over polka-dot embossing template and run stylus across surface. Emboss another Eyelet Charm flower in upper right corner of scored square of cardstock and lightly sand raised surfaces. Attach to front of folder.

BEST FRIENDS
by Loni Stevens

Button, jigsaw alphabet, mini brads,
patterned cardstock, ribbon,
scrapbook colors acrylic paint,
stitches and woven label:
Making Memories
Embossing powder: Ranger Industries
Photo turns: 7Gypsies
Punches: EK Success and Paper Shapers
Stamping ink: VersaMagic by Tsukineko

how to: Cut a strip of patterned cardstock, randomly punch small flower shapes along the strip and ink edges. Cover solid side of strip with clear embossing powder, heat emboss and repeat for a second coat. Attach strip across top of layout and add a ribbon below, stitching to secure. Punch large flower from patterned cardstock, heat emboss two layers of embossing powder to solid side, zigzag stitch around petals and add button for center.

A TIME TO GROW
by Robin Johnson

Alphabet stamps: PSX Design

Brads, cardstock and label holder:
Making Memories

Paper: 7Gypsies and Daisy D's

Stamping ink: Ranger Industries

how to: Create stripes on the right edge of background paper using a variety of patterned papers and cardstock. Attach using various sewing machine stitches. Create a second set of the same pattern to use for the title. Use a template or computer-printed letters to trace and cut out letters from the second set and attach along bottom border. Create photo mat by layering different sizes, patterns and colors of paper and secure with sewing machine stitching. Add photo, journaling and stamped words along striped border. Ink edges to finish.

SCHOOL BUS
by Maggie Holmes

Hinges, leather frame, leather photo corners, ledger paper, mailbox alphabet, patterned cardstock, petite signage, ribbon, safety pin and staples: Making Memories

Paper: Design Originals

Stamping ink: Ranger Industries

Other: Charm, jewelry tag and tulle

how to: Measure and cut various coordinating patterned papers and cardstock and zigzag stitch together to create a quilted background. Wrap a wide strip of tulle around the middle and add photos, embellishments and journaling on top.

SWAK
by Robin Johnson

Alphabet stamps: Hampton Art

Buttons, cardstock, jump rings, ribbon
and snaps: Making Memories

Envelopes: Hero Arts

Paper: Daisy D's

Stamping ink: Ranger Industries

Other: Lace, suede ribbon
and watercolor paint

how to: Fold background paper every inch on both diagonals and color with watercolors or dye. Let paper dry and iron to flatten. Accordion-fold a strip of patterned paper, ink both sides of the folds and attach across bottom of background. Cut photo mat and fold all edges. Ink creases, lay flat, attach lace across bottom and adhere mat to background, slightly overlapping paper strip. Stamp title onto envelopes and string together with jump rings.

PICTURE PERFECT
by Julie Turner

Cardstock tag, decorative brad, mini brads, patterned cardstock, scrapbook colors acrylic paint and scrapbook dye: Making Memories

Other: Chipboard, corner punch and ribbon

how to: Create an embossing template with a rectangular piece of chipboard slightly larger than the photo. Lightly tape to front of layout, turn over and emboss around edges. Remove chipboard to reveal recessed photo mat. Create flower by fringing three 3-inch strips of cardstock and/or patterned cardstock. Dye strips and paint edges as desired. Trim the fringe from two of the strips so that petals will be graduated. Layer together, with the shortest in the middle, and roll. Holding the end, carefully fold down the petals and secure with glue and a Decorative Brad. Attach to layout.

gallery

ARTISTS
AND
AUTHOR

LILAC CHANG
San Mateo, California

As the mother of two boys and, most recently, a girl, Lilac suddenly finds herself and her layouts exploding with flowers, ribbon, pink and all things feminine. It's an entirely different world but she's loving it. When it comes to paper, she's loving layering, stitching and distressing to create a look all her own.

MAGGIE HOLMES
South Jordan, Utah

Maggie absolutely cannot live without her digital camera, diet strawberry limeade from Sonic, frequent trips to Arizona and an ever-expanding collection of shoes. She is a Mac girl through and through—with her computer and makeup preferences—and she loves adding as much ribbon as possible to any and all kinds of paper.

JENNIFER JENSEN
Hurricane, Utah

Jennifer can't say "no" to sitting poolside sipping a frozen Coke, a fresh new hair color every six weeks and riding the roller coaster at least 20 times on the annual Jensen family pilgrimage to Disneyland. When it comes to paper, she always says "yes" to cutting and trimming it to create one-of-a-kind embellishments.

LONI STEVENS
Pleasant Grove, Utah

She hates to admit it, but Loni gets more excited shopping for new art supplies than shopping for new clothes. And she never misses an episode of Oprah—she watches it religiously. Her favorite thing to do with paper is stamp on it with her alphabet stamp collection—nearly eighty sets of them at last count!

ERIN TERRELL
San Antonio, Texas

At dinnertime, you'll most likely find Erin at P.F. Chang's sporting L'Oréal's Headstrong on her fingers and toes. Later, at home, she'll snack on Nestle Toll House Cookie Bars while burning an Apricot and Honey-scented Yankee Candle. All while mixing and matching her extensive stash of paper to create unique color combinations.

JULIE TURNER
Gilbert, Arizona

Between traveling to exotic places and home schooling her two children, it's a wonder Julie finds time to scrapbook! With everything going on, you'll often find an experiment of some sort happening at the Turner house. Lately, she's been caught red, blue, green and pink-handed while perfecting her new favorite thing to do with paper—dyeing.

JENNIFER KOFFORD AUTHOR
Ogden, Utah

Constantly on the go, when Jennifer has a minute of spare time, you'll most likely find her watching "Alias", reality-TV or an old movie, reading home-decorating magazines, power shopping or planning her next dream vacation. Although not her favorite thing to do with paper, she most often finds herself writing on it.

CONTRIBUTING ARTISTS

WENDY ANDERSON
Heber City, Utah

HILLARY BEVAN
Concord, California

JOY BOHAN
Bedford, Indiana

JOANNA BOLICK
Fletcher, North Carolina

CHARLA CAMPBELL
Rogerville, Missouri

JANET HOPKINS
Frisco, Texas

KIM HUGHES
Binghampton, New York

ROBIN JOHNSON
Farmington, Utah

LISA MCGARVEY
Vista, California

JAYME SHEPHERD
Providence, Utah

ROBYN WERLICH
Lehi, Utah

KARA WYLIE
Frisco, Texas

be inspired.